MW01531717

GIVING CAN
HURT

LET'S MOVE PEOPLE TO
SELF-SUFFICIENCY

DEAN H. CURTIS

interweave*solutions*.org

GIVING HAS IMPACT!

I believe in giving. When natural disasters happen, our donations help people get back on their feet. Giving to schools, churches, NGOs and other good causes can create hope, increase knowledge, provide opportunities and relieve the poverty of others.

But giving can also **hurt.** It can damage people's chances of overcoming long term poverty.

For example, Frederick is one of the hundreds of thousands of unemployed in Zimbabwe. He finished high school. He is in his late twenties, shy and lacks confidence and vision. He and his friends hang out in the street and play video games when they get any extra money.

He begs for money in the marketplace and asks for money at his church. He doesn't look for a job or start a business because he can survive on what he is given and in his mind he has no hope for change.

Sofia from Colombia is one of the millions of people buying and selling in the street to survive. She didn't complete primary school and is now in her late fifties.

She sells fruit. Her house is full of fruit pulp that has been frozen and put into plastic bags. She has joined a Masters of Business in the Street (MBS) self-reliance group and is learning for the first time how to keep records, grow and formalize her business.

Fredrick and Sofia both provide for themselves. One asks for handouts while the other works to become self-sufficient.

Giving to someone to meet an immediate need is uncomplicated. We see someone in need and we give. We feel good and they get short-term relief.

Giving in order to help a person become self-sufficient is much harder. Hope, motivation, knowledge and support are needed by people trying to create their own income or find employment.

This book is written for two groups of people: Those who want to give money or means to help people help themselves, and those who want to give of their time to work directly with others who are trying to become self-sufficient.

Thousands of people all over the world are becoming more self-sufficient because of wise contributions of time and money from people like you.

Welcome to a new way to give.

Give for self-sufficiency.

To Julie Curtis

For raising our nine children and caring for my elderly mother while I visit developing countries around the world. You have made this book possible.

Cover photo by David Curtis

At Interweave Solutions we respect everyone who has worked with us to fight poverty — and especially those who are working on self–reliance in their own lives. So while the stories in this book are true, names and images may have been altered, characters combined and details changed to protect privacy and better illustrate the self–reliance principles.

CONTENTS

WHY DO WE GIVE?

∞∞∞∞∞∞∞∞∞∞∞∞∞∞∞∞

A lady with cracked lips and a hardened face approached me on a snowy night during the Christmas season. She was obviously cold and homeless, and she was asking me for money. I was just outside Temple Square, the city block in Salt Lake City, Utah, USA where the Church of Jesus Christ of Latter-Day Saints landmark temple is located and where there is usually someone looking for a handout.

"I should give her something." I thought. Why? Was it guilt because I have money and a home and she doesn't? Was it spiritual promptings because of the holiday or location? Was it annoyance because she was bothering me when I wanted to get out of the cold and into my car? I couldn't describe exactly why, but something said I needed to help, I needed to give.

I felt I needed to do more than hand her some change. I got her to an inexpensive hotel where I paid her room for a night and gave her some money for food. I had gotten her out of the cold and she had food to eat.

As I drove home listening to Christmas music and noticing the Christmas lights, I still didn't know if I felt glad or relieved or maybe even still a little annoyed.

I forgot about it.

I moved from the area, but six years later I came back to visit Temple Square. I was approached again by someone asking for money. As I looked closely I realized it was the same woman from six years ago! She was even more weather worn now and it was summer, but she was still homeless, still hungry and still asking for money.

This time I recognized my feelings. I felt mad at myself for giving so much money and time years ago. I was mad at her for not changing. It bothered me that hundreds of people like me had given her money for the last six years, thinking it might make a difference. I was confused about what I should do at that moment and in the future when I'd be asked to give again.

Six years earlier I had relieved short-term suffering for one night but had not solved any long-term poverty. I had not helped the woman in any way to be more self-sufficient. In some ways, I, along with hundreds of others, had made it so she didn't have to make any changes or seek long-term help. Had I helped for one night and hurt her future in the process?

HOW CAN WE GIVE TO HELP LONG-TERM SELF-SUFFICIENCY?

I have two colleagues, Rocio "Chio" Lizano, and Jay Bosshardt, who have helped me develop a better philosophy regarding how to give for greater impact.

Chio is married to a prosperous accountant in Quito, Ecuador. She raises four children, cares for their two dogs, participates in her daughter's soccer league and helps hundreds of people become more self-reliant as a Success Ambassador for Interweave Solutions.

I saw her in action on a steep mountainside in Quito. Chio cheerfully greeted the eight participants that were attending her self-reliance group that day. It didn't matter that some were slow learners, some couldn't read and some were physically handicapped. They were there with their caregivers to learn how they could become more self-sufficient and start or improve their own micro-businesses. They were not there for handouts.

She has formed similar groups in the past. These groups of 5 to 20 people meet together often to learn business concepts, support and encourage each other and improve their income, homes and communities. Sometimes these groups are sponsored by government agencies, micro-finance institutions, or churches. Sometimes it's just a group of neighbors. Currently, she is working with the Quito national police and their spouses so that the families have a more sustainable retirement someday and the police won't be as susceptible to bribes.

Jay Bosshardt grew up as part of a family owned operation, a salt mine in central Utah, United States. His father had discovered a geological formation beneath their hay fields that contained large quantities of salt.

The family developed the mine and Jay worked there for most of his life helping turn it into a successful enterprise that now sells their unique salt brand all over the world.

When the family sold the mine, Jay had money and the desire to help others, particularly in developing countries. He visited non-profit organizations and went on several humanitarian expeditions. However, when he helped build another school or visited another orphanage he wondered how these good people would ever become self-sufficient and not always be dependent on the help and donations of others.

Jay wanted his gifts to change the way the people he helped **thought** about poverty and self-sufficiency. How could he encourage them to be more self-reliant and not just depend on donations? He kept looking until he found an approach to giving that focused on self-sufficiency.

He traveled to South America and saw for himself that local Ecuadorians and Colombians could help each other create micro-businesses and become more self-reliant through groups. He learned that local groups around the world were helping people to create business, home and community action plans. They didn't need visitors from the north to solve their problems.

Now some of his donations go to recruit, train and support local Success Ambassadors all over the world who organize and facilitate self-reliance groups. In these groups, people teach and support each other in order to increase their income, improve their homes and serve their communities. The primary focus of his giving now is helping others learn basic skills and behaviors congruent with a productive and self-reliant life.

Helping people become self-sufficient is not easy. Giving can actually discourage self-sufficiency if not done correctly. Sometimes giving helps, but sometimes it can hurt. This book will help you recognize the difference.

OUR HISTORY: HOW DO WE GIVE BACK?

Our family's Thanksgiving dinners are often served along with a friendly exchange on how best to eliminate world poverty.

"The only way we are going to reduce poverty in foreign countries is through business development." I used to assert. "Health, human rights, literacy are all great but if there is no money or business, there is still poverty."

My brother, Lynn, would disagree. "Business means profit motives. A society can't get ahead if everyone is always thinking about money." He would respond. "Social development is the only way to reduce poverty long term."

"Sing kumbaya all you want," I retorted. "You can have all of the social development in the world but ultimately people need incomes. That means business."

I had decided that business development was the only way of reducing poverty in the world. My older brother on the other hand, had decided that it was charitable international development that would be the world's best hope of ending economic disparity and poverty.

MY HISTORY OF BUSINESS

Palos Verdes, California has great brownies. The one I had on July 15, 2000, at 11:30 a.m. was probably the best I have ever bought. It was the first purchase I made as a millionaire.

Earlier that day, in the plush office surroundings of the Long Beach World Trade Center, I completed a two-year negotiation by signing the papers to give ownership of my fifteen-year-old company, Curtis and Associates, Inc., to AFSA, a company owned by Fleet Boston Bank.

Curtis and Associates, Inc., a consulting firm that eventually grew to have over five hundred employees, worked with Departments of Social Services nationwide to find jobs for people receiving welfare.

We created employment resource centers. With a motivating curriculum, we trained welfare recipients to find work and provided computers, phones, fax machines, and a supportive environment to help them succeed. In many of our contracts, we were paid only if the person found a job. During the fifteen years of business, we saw thousands of people solve their own poverty problems by finding and keeping a job.

But the time had come to sell the business. After two years of negotiation and work, we completed the complicated sale.

With the stroke of the pen, I suddenly had millions of dollars in cash and over three million in a charity advised fund that I could direct to any cause of my choice.

In two more years, I had completed my employment contract with AFSA, and in January of 2002, I suddenly found myself completely free of work obligations and with access to millions of dollars.

Now, what would you do?

Most would say, "Whatever I want!"

I did. For a few weeks I took long hot baths, read the paper from cover to cover each morning, and tried not to bother my wife. I decompressed.

And then I asked myself the question, "What next?"

I dusted off some old dreams. In July of 2002, after moving closer to extended family in Layton, Utah, I took three of my four boys (my fourth was too young) on a month-long bike trip from Canada to Mexico. Camping out, spending time with the boys, and enjoying the beautiful Pacific coastline was a father's dream come true.

Returning with a farmer's tan, stronger leg muscles, and great family memories, I soon asked the question again, "Now what?"

Within a few months, the question was answered when I received an invitation from my church to serve the local congregations in Tampico, Mexico for three years with my family.

The "now what" question was temporarily answered. For the next three years, my wife and I had the sublime experience of dedicating our lives to serving God and our fellow men in Mexico. Living in a developing country provided powerful experiences that helped form a philosophy of what I should and should not do to reduce poverty.

I remember on one occasion a man called me from the United States wanting to give away some hygiene kits that consisted of toothpaste, shampoo, soap, and washcloths. I contacted a leader of a local church in the small town of San Felipe, asking whether any members of his congregation would want some hygiene kits.

I remember him scratching his head and asking why anyone would want to give him and his congregation toothbrushes and soap. He finally agreed to it and decided to distribute the kits when I brought them the next time I was in town.

We unpacked the kits and put them in his office, and then he asked, a little confused, "Why does anyone want to give away some toothpaste and soap? Do they think we don't have soap? Or do they think we don't know how to use a toothbrush?"

I assured him that people were just trying to be friendly, but it did seem to be a solution looking for a problem.

That sort of thing happened regularly. Well-meaning people would bring supplies to areas that didn't need or ask for those supplies. Of course, the people take the free "stuff," but they often wondered why others were giving away silly things. Some of these families and small villages even became dependent on the regular supplies that would come from the "helpful" foreign families.

A generous couple sent used computers and supplies to a small village in the mountains of Mexico. They gave the computers to one family in the small church congregation. Other families in the congregation became jealous, and the arrival of computers and supplies from the north caused major divisions in the small group, and eventually several families quit coming to the church.

In Mexico, I saw poverty for the first time from a new perspective. I was rubbing shoulders and working with some people that lived in cardboard houses with plastic roofs. Yet they were happy, intelligent, and contributing members of their community. I got to know personally many people I had only thought of and seen in the past as "poor Mexicans."

Now I knew Francisco, his wife and three children by name. He and his family, and others like him, had talents, dreams, and ideas on how to improve their own lives. Many needed help and training, but they didn't need handouts. When they were organized and empowered with ideas and knowledge, they could solve their own local and community challenges.

Knowing people in a developing country changed my perspective on poverty. After returning home from Mexico, I began to ask again, "So, what can I do?," but by then I knew that the answer had to include more than just giving away "stuff." I decided the answer to poverty in developing nations was business.

MY BROTHER AND CHARITABLE COMMUNITY DEVELOPMENT

Lynn is three years older than I am and tells exotic stories. He can. He has visited over sixty-five countries in his international development career. Upon graduating from Brigham Young University in 1977, Lynn moved to Syracuse, New York, and began to work for Laubach Literacy. There he began a career that led him to implement reading and functional literacy programs worldwide.

Eight years prior to his move to New York, Lynn had served in Taiwan and Hong Kong for his church. He saw extreme poverty. On one occasion, as he was swept through a crowded sidewalk in a humble area of Hong Kong, he bumped into a large cardboard box next to a building on a busy sidewalk. The press of the crowd made it impossible to avoid, and as he brushed along its side, he was able to glance in. There he saw a young mother, crouched in the cardboard box, holding and trying to comfort a small baby. As the mother looked up, Lynn saw that she had blood matted about her face. Her eyes seemed to implore, "Please, help. I have nothing, and nowhere to go."

The crowd pushed him forward, but the mental picture had been taken. He stumbled on, the cardboard box disappearing in the bustling crowd. But at that moment his life changed. He consciously decided that he must work in the nonprofit sector, helping to relieve poverty.

Laubach Literacy was a perfect launching pad for his future career. While completing a Ph.D. at Syracuse University in adult learning, Lynn designed a teaching approach to adult literacy that involved working with people at the local level in developing countries so that they could obtain functional literacy. He refers to this teaching model as FAMA; an acronym that stands for Facts, Association, Meaning and Action. With this learning methodology, he works with groups all over the world to motivate them to develop their own solutions.

He discovered that adults want to solve their own problems, and health, income, and home issues were more important to adults than sitting in a classroom learning to read. If people identified a personal problem and then saw how learning to read could help them resolve the issue, then they were motivated to learn to read. Lynn wasn't as successful when he came in and said, "Here are some literacy classes." Few adults would attend.

Over the years, he experienced many adventures as he honed his unique teaching model of self-motivation. Robbery at gunpoint, malaria in Uganda, and prison in Panama for organizing people were all part of Lynn's learning process. This led to understanding learner motivation as an integral part of international development.

At many family gatherings, we would discuss poverty and how to overcome it. Lynn was always very community development-focused, and I was very keen on business. From my perspective, without a job or a productive form of income, people could never lift themselves out of poverty. The economic development of nations through vibrant business was the way we would reduce poverty in the world.

"No," he would reply. "Business is about profit. A profit motive causes exploitation. If we can't teach them to read and solve their own local problems, then poverty will never be solved."

"They can read all they want," I would respond. "One of the biggest local problems is that there are no jobs. That means that it doesn't matter how well they read—they still have no money for food. They will still live in cardboard boxes if they have no viable means of income. Someone has to create the jobs, or there will still be poverty."

So, every Thanksgiving, the friendly arguement of how to solve world poverty emerged, with business at one end and charity at the other. Both of us were attacking poverty. In the United States, I was creating jobs and helping people on welfare find employment. Internationally, Lynn was helping people learn to read and establish local groups to resolve neighborhood issues. We each were slowly developing an approach to help people become self-sufficient.

I didn't want to just give money or time to the many organizations that helped the poor. I had seen that often times, giving could actually work against the idea of helping others become self-sufficient. I wanted to find something that would not cause harm.

Finally, after deciding to working together, my brother and I organized a nonprofit organization to help people become self-sufficient. We called it Interweave Solutions.

GIVING CAN HURT

◇◇◇◇◇◇◇◇◇◇◇◇◇◇◇◇◇◇

As a young man, I used to think there was no harm in giving. However, I have since learned that if we follow the adage "give till it hurts," we might not have to give for very long. Giving can hurt. It can cause arrogance in the giver and dependency in the receiver. It can also destroy jobs.

ARROGANCE

My Boy Scouts of America Eagle project when I was seventeen years old was a clothing and toys drive for a poor village in Mexico. I motivated my friends at South Torrance High School in Southern California to bring used clothing and toys to a drop off point. I loaded the donations in the back of a pickup truck, and my buddy and I headed across the border to a small town south of Tijuana.

We didn't really know anyone in the village. We just drove down the old dirt road to the main plaza area and parked the truck. The village was really hot, dirty, and poor compared to my standard of living.

Giving out stuff for an Eagle Scout Project (1970)

We thought, "How do we give this stuff out? People are obviously poor and could use what we have. What do we do now?"

By this time, we were a curiosity in the small village. People began to gather around the truck and wonder why we were there. We finally climbed in the back of the truck, looked at each other and said, "Let's get started!" We started handing out the stuff. Soon other villagers saw that there was free stuff and came running to the truck. We were quickly surrounded by people clamoring for anything that was free.

As the crowd got bigger, we didn't know what to do, so we began to just throw the stuff out of the truck, and the people just grabbed for it. It was a feeding frenzy for a few moments. Everyone took something free, and then it was over. There were a few kids looking at some old baseball gloves with confusion, so we got out of the truck, helped them figure out how to use the gloves, played some baseball for a few hours, and then went home.

Baseball with the village kids in Mexico (1970)

On a basic level, we should have been congratulated as teenagers who saw poverty and acted. But on the other hand, we had no idea whether there was a used clothing salesman in the village that we may have just driven out of business by flooding the market with used clothes. We didn't know if maybe someone was learning how to be a seamstress, and we ruined her incentive because free clothes came from an ignorant donor. After all, why learn a skill when stuff just shows up?

Our good intentions could have been economically harmful, but I didn't know that as a teenager. What I did know is that I had, and they didn't. I gave and they received. I solidified in my mind that these people were needy, and I felt good when I gave.

I came home with pictures and stories of the poverty and of my benevolence. I got my Eagle Scout badge. But I didn't learn about people. I just learned that I felt important when I gave.

Frequently, we are exposed to pictures of dirty children living in shacks in developing countries from an organization asking for money. We are touched by the photos and are often motivated to give. We write the check and feel good about helping to solve poverty.

They need; we give. They are weak; we are strong. They are impoverished; we are not. Whatever we give, they are grateful to receive.

After living with the wonderful people of Mexico for three years, I can only imagine what the people in that village must have thought after our frenzied distribution: "Those crazy gringos. Drive in, dump a bunch of stuff, and leave."

"If they want to give away stuff, I'll take it," I imagined them saying. "But I have no clue why. Do they think we don't have clothes?"

I know what I thought. "Poor Mexicans need us to come down and solve their problems."

Living in Mexico four decades later helped me see things from the perspective of the Mexicans. They are willing to receive things, but it doesn't solve long-term problems and can even hurt.

That is true worldwide. As the Peruvian business magazine *Caretas* writes, "more than help, what we need [in Peru] are partners" (Prada, F. 2012, March 8. *¿Ayuda para el Perú?* Caretas, 2222).

For me, the lesson was simple. Help people identify and solve their own problems. When we attempt to solve a problem in our own way and from our North American perspective, we often just fuel our own arrogance.

However, we can do some real damage as well.

DEPENDENCY

What would have happened if, in my Eagle Scout project, we had promised to come back every six months with another batch of clothes? What if this had not been a one-time visit? If we had been committed to the village?

That could have been worse.

I have seen villages become dependent on donors to find a teacher for the school, fix the water pump, provide the school supplies, and solve the problems.

Almost all of us have seen citizens become dependent on government programs, people dependent on church aid, and villages dependent on nonprofit agencies. Instead of solving their own problems, they wait to see what the government, church, or nonprofit organization is going to do.

It is human nature to accept stuff. If that stuff comes without a price or an effort, and it comes regularly, then we can easily become dependent on it. Once dependency occurs, attitudes of entitlement soon follow.

I deserve the help. I really am poor.

If you were really Christians, you would help more. Don't you know that I can't live on what you give me?

How come they don't help us like they help the other village? We have to really show how poor we are if we want to get outside money or support.

I remember doing a self-sufficiency workshop in Mozambique. I asked everyone in the group to dress for a job search the next day. One of the men arrived with dirty, ripped clothing. He was unshaven and had his small child.

I was confused as to why he looked so poor. He explained, "I thought we were going job searching today. I want the employers to know that I am poor and really need a job. I hope they feel sorry for me."

When people feel powerless, they hope others will give them a way out– perhaps a well, some food, clothing, or even a job. Ignorant giving teaches them to think about how they can get others to provide them with short-term solutions, instead of thinking how they can improve the situation themselves.

Generosity without self-reliance principles can cause dependency and it can also destroy opportunity.

DESTROY JOBS AND LOCAL ECONOMIES

Ever since my living in Mexico experience, I have worked with hundreds of micro-businesses in developing countries. From used clothing to reading glasses, tortillas to bananas, each business struggles to start up and get customers. I have also seen the destruction of businesses by charity.

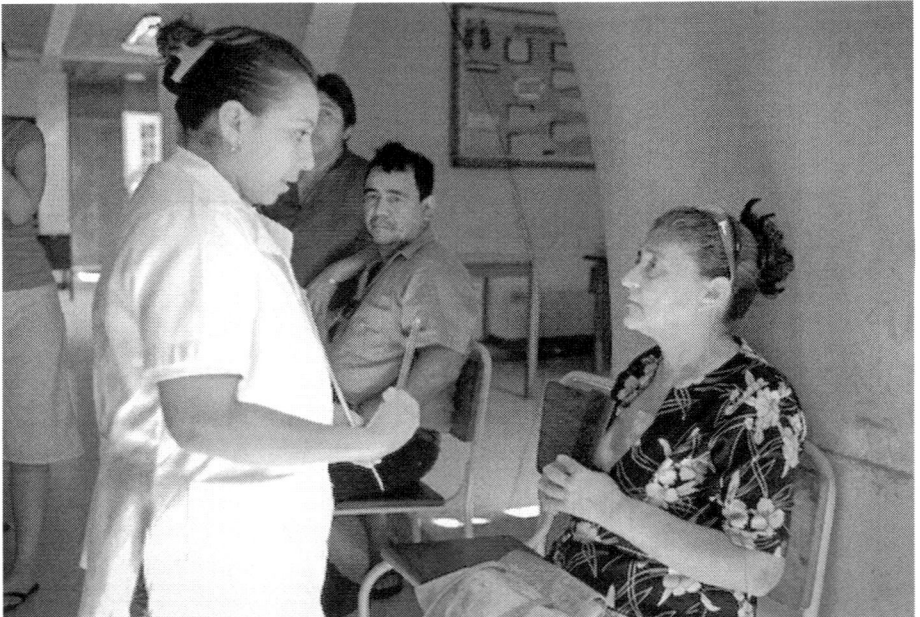

Nicaragua women giving an eye exam while selling eyeglasses

I was working with a group of women in Nicaragua who established a small business selling reading glasses. They helped their clients choose the magnification level of the reading glasses and educated their customers about presbyopia, a condition in which the lens of the eye loses its ability to focus, making it difficult to see objects up close. It eventually affects everyone according to the *A.D.A.M. Medical Encyclopedia*. Most people notice it when they start wishing they had longer arms to be able to move the reading material farther away, and it usually happens between forty to fifty years of age. It is a simple problem to solve with an inexpensive pair of reading glasses.

However, if you don't know about presbyopia, you might think that your eyes are uniquely going bad and you need a professional eye exam with expensive prescription glasses. In a developing country, that means many people have to give up reading or using their hands for detail work like sewing or engine repair because they can no longer focus and can't afford expensive exams and prescription glasses.

These eyeglass entrepreneurs offered an important service, education, and an inexpensive source of reading glasses. All was going well with the sales of the glasses until a benevolent donor from a more developed country decided to help the community by giving away three thousand pairs of eyeglasses. On a special give-away day, the village showed up, and thousands left as proud owners of free reading glasses.

The small business owners suddenly had no market. No one wanted to buy what comes free. Needing work and feeling discouraged, each one left the reading glasses business, and the market shut down. However, months later, with new people having eye problems, broken glasses, and the need for more education, the village had no source for inexpensive eye education and reading glasses. What was an act of extreme kindness and charity months earlier destroyed jobs and cut off a long-term service for the community. The generosity left the village worse off in the long run.

In *The Wall Street Journal*, on March 9, 2009, Dambisa Moyo complains about how aid has kept Africa poor and gives a similar example with mosquito nets. When the nets are given away, the market and the jobs are destroyed. Later, when the people need more nets, they have no source except to beg for more nets from an outside agency. He explains that the same thing happens at the national level. When nations receive mass donations of used clothing, eye glasses, doctor care etc. without proper technical and business training, the foreign aid actually ruins the local markets and creates unemployment because the free supplies and services compete against local providers.

I have learned that if we are not careful, giving can cause arrogance and dependency. It can also destroy jobs.

However, business and giving can work together. In fact, they must be interwoven to really address poverty. With the right methodology, we really can give for impact.

GIVING FOR IMPACT

I think we all want to help solve the poverty and injustice in the world, but we just don't know how. When do we give? Will money help?

We are offered many ways to give on a regular basis. Many nonprofit organizations offer food, hot meals, clean water, school buildings, or disaster relief. Often, friends who always seem to be in trouble ask for help. These charities are valuable and should be supported, and these friends may be needy, but always remember the importance of self-sufficiency.

In order to determine whether your help or donation encourages self-sufficiency, you can ask two important questions:

1. *Does the donation help or encourage some sort of income generation?*

2. *Is the recipient of the donation, to the extent possible, asked to work, contribute to, or purchase something to receive the service?*

Do you, or the nonprofit organization you want to donate to, encourage income generation?

Disasters happen. Our donations of money and time to help with hurricane or earthquake victims are life-saving. Please be generous when obvious short-term needs must be met.

However, be careful of giveaway charities or handouts after the immediate need is met. Even though they provide much needed immediate relief, they can have a long-term disruptive effect on income generation.

Whether it be reading glasses, mosquito nets, or used clothing, if a well-meaning organization or individual gives away products or services without thinking about how the recipient will earn a living in the future, it often creates a longer-term problem of dependency.

I remember talking to a seamstress of thirty years in El Salvador who was trying to create a new business not related to sewing because she said she could not compete with the flood of used clothes on the market. Charity had destroyed her business.

Doctors have often given services for free. They will go into a village and perform life-saving operations. They must be encouraged, however, to think about the income-generation component when they leave.

In a poor area of Port-au-Prince, a European NGO came and offered free medical services for about a year. Everyone was excited about the high quality of care from the Europeans. Any local doctors in the area could not compete against the free care offered, and they left that section of the city. A year later the Europeans pulled out of Haiti. The area was left without local health care, and the people in the neighborhood were at the mercy of government or international NGOs to solve their local problem. Charity had caused dependency and destroyed local initiative.

The European doctor group should have had a focus on training local doctors with not only medical practices but also with business ideas for how to provide these services when they were gone. Perhaps they could have helped local doctors price their services, promote the services, and improve the local processes. They could have worked with the local doctors to develop a long-term growth plan.

Please, in your donating, look for organizations that have an income-generating component. Is there small business training? Is there a micro-lending fund? Is there local leadership and involvement in the project? All of these are important questions when looking for a donation that will make a long-term impact on self-reliance.

When working with a friend or relative, have the discussion about long-term solutions. Perhaps make the person commit to attending a career workshop, self-reliance group or register at workforce services as a condition of receiving your help.

Do you or the nonprofit organization you donate to invite the recipients to work, contribute to, or purchase, the product or service?

Another harmful result of just giving away nets or glasses or medicine is that it often goes unappreciated or unused. If the recipient hasn't gone through the thought process of the value of a net and made the sacrifice to purchase one, then he or she often puts it to the side and neglects it.

I visited a home of a family in drought-stricken Ethiopia. A well-meaning NGO had built a rain collection system with a 500-gallon tank on a poor woman's farm. When we visited, the connection from the roof to the gallon container was missing. She had taken the spout for another use. The collection system was inoperative one month after installation. She had not processed the value of the water collection system and had not participated in its development. She was pleased that some outsider had come and done some work on the farm, but she had not put in any effort to make the system succeed.

Any behavior change, whether it is wearing glasses, sleeping in nets, or collecting water in a new way, needs to be accepted and processed by the local villager. There has to be a "conversion" to the idea. Selling a product or service is an excellent way to create buy-in. An economic transaction offers an opportunity for the purchaser to commit to the product or service. The person has to be educated enough to understand the purchase and committed enough to make the purchase.

If we encourage local villagers to sell goods and services at reasonable prices and teach them how to make a profit in the process, then we have a win-win-win situation. Jobs are created, services in the community are provided, and end-users are persuaded and committed to use the product.

What if the person doesn't have the money to pay? This is often true of an education, a well, a house, or other larger ticket items. In this case, offering some form of meaningful work or service as a "payment" is an important part of self-reliance. The recipient should help dig the latrine, help gather the people, sell the glasses, provide referrals, or give leadership. The local participant needs to do all he or she can to "purchase" or earn the product or service.

The local villagers asking for latrines, schools, books, or water wells should also be able to explain their local commitment to the project. Do they have a local leadership council that is advocating for the project? Are they encouraging local participation? Are they requiring local commitment?

I was talking to an engineer who wanted to make a difference in the world. He went on a service expedition to Africa. He found himself in a hole digging a new latrine next to another professional businessman who was digging with him. They looked around and saw the villagers watching the curious sight of the two white men digging the hole. He suddenly realized that the one thing that these villagers could offer in this project was labor. They had time, curiosity, and ability to dig a hole, yet they stood around watching.

Self-reliance is fostered when we challenge and invite the recipients to do as much of the planning, work, and implementation as possible.

This is true closer to home as well.

When giving money to a friend or family member, try to ask them to do something in return. Maybe they can develop a family budget, clean their own kitchen, or help you with some yard work before they receive the money they need or want. Help them do all they can to earn or work for the donation.

Obviously there are other things to consider when a stranger asks for money on the street.

I rarely give money to strangers and I don't feel guilty if I am giving time and money to self-sufficiency organizations following the previous guidelines. However, there may be times when you feel moved to help a stranger in need.

Here are some suggestions:

1. Buy what they are asking for instead of giving money. It takes more time and more money to buy a lunch rather than giving some change but you will know that you gave them what they needed.

2. Mentally give one dollar more to the organization of your choice. In your mind you say, "I choose to give, just not to you at this time."

3. Give a business card of a local shelter or food pantry.

4. Keep a bag of oranges or granola bars in your car and give them food instead of money.

5. On rare occasions, give them money if you really feel impressed to do so and confident it will help. I'm not asking you to be cruel but to be smart.

When we lived in Mexico, we had people coming to our house asking for something on a regular basis. We looked for ways for them to work. Often, we let them wash the car and we tried to buy their products if they were selling something.

When they had no product or we had no work, we would often give them a small food bag my wife had prepared in advance instead of money. It didn't cause self-sufficiency and it didn't give them a source of income either. It fed them for a day. That's the least we could do.

So in review, when deciding whether to give to a project or organization, two good questions to ask are:

1. *Does this charity help the people being served to generate their own income?*

2. *Is this donation challenging the recipients to work or contribute to improve their own cause?*

THINK SELF-RELIANCE!

Interweave Solutions is our non-profit organization we created in 2008 to help people become self-sufficient. Over the years we have developed a system creating self-sufficiency groups through what we call Success Ambassadors.

We pioneered this model years ago in Ecuador with several local congregations of the Church of Jesus Christ of Latter Day Saints. We established a self-reliance group in several of their congregations and invited all of the members to attend.

The self-reliance groups provided service projects to orphanages, cleaned up streets, and started businesses. Participants achieved goals such as better family communication, losing weight, and continuing education. In addition to strengthening existing businesses and starting their own new micro-businesses, over a hundred new jobs were created, and many of them were shared with other group members.

Interweave was asked to serve on a self-reliance committee in Salt Lake City, Utah to help the Church develop materials they could use around the world to establish self-reliance groups. After years of pilots and collaboration, the Church of Jesus Christ of Latter Day Saints has developed its own self-reliance materials and offers self-reliance groups worldwide to its thousands of congregations. Nearly a million people have participated in self-reliance groups in chapels around the world.

We are now offering the Masters of Business in the Streets (MBS) self-reliance group model to churches of all faiths, as well as government agencies, micro-finance institutions and neighborhoods around the world.

A Church self-reliance group in Guyana

The following chapters explain how the MBS program works and how people can become Success Ambassadors. It is a powerful example of giving that is creating self-sufficiency all over the world.

THE MASTERS OF BUSINESS IN THE STREET (MBS)

Deborah, an MBS participant in the Congo

Deborah is one of the 70% of the population of the Democratic Republic of the Congo who suffers from food insecurity even though she has a micro-business. She buys and sells fish, charcoal and biscuits. Deborah's business is part of the informal economy (buyers and sellers in the street that pay no taxes and have neither government support nor permission) and is just one example of the need to think about giving differently.

A study for the *Results for Development Institute* explains the informal economy as, *"primarily comprised of self-employed people working from home or street-vending. They have neither official nor permanent places of business. ...Typically the incomes of informal workers are low and are also unpredictable. In many developing countries the informal economy is the main source of employment for as many as 9 out of every 10 workers,"* (Pina, P., Kotin, T., Hausman, V., & Macharia, E. (2012). Skills for Employability: The Informal Economy. Innovative Secondary Education for Skills Enhancement.). In other words, as many as 90% of all workers in some countries live off the unreliable revenue from their own informal business.

There are over 2.15 billion people in the informal economy trying to make ends meet by buying and selling (micro-business) in the street. Many have only a primary education. Some can barely read and write. Many workers live in remote villages with no access to formal education. Those in the city often have no access to an adequate education, let alone business training.

How can we get affordable, usable training to the masses in the informal economy? If they can succeed in their micro-businesses, they can solve their own poverty and help others become self-sufficient. Successful businesses create jobs.

We are certainly not reaching the informal economy now.

The *Results for Development Institute* also states *"... school- based education and training programs **seldom penetrate the informal economy**, resulting in weak cognitive skills in most informal workers."*

In addition to most training programs, *"...where they do exist, too often [the focus is] solely on technical skills without integrating non-cognitive skills. Across industries, abilities to communicate effectively, organize efficiently, and solve unanticipated problems are desired, and often required, in a valuable worker."*

The study concluded, *"...workers who remain informally-employed would benefit greatly from improved business and entrepreneurial skills,"* (Pina, Kotin, Hausman, & Macharia 2012).

My review on the Internet revealed a lot of options for small business training in developed countries but practically nothing for businesses in the informal economy.

There is a solution: **Masters of Business in the Street (MBS)/Self-Reliance Groups.**

When Deborah joined the Interweave Masters of Business in the Street (MBS) self-reliance group in the Congo, she knew she needed to have more customers to make more money, but she wasn't sure how she could do so.

"Thank you for offering support and training," she told us. "This is my only source of income. I am working hard but I need help."

Part of the help Deborah received was in understanding that she could advertise her products in other areas of her neighborhood. After learning about promotion, one of the six principles of business taught in the MBS self-reliance program, Deborah found a few pieces of cardboard and began to make signs advertising her fish and biscuits. Traffic increased to her stall and she was able to buy fresher fish, resulting in even more customers.

Where in the formal business world will the professors teach or even permit someone launching a marketing plan to use cardboard and borrowed markers?

With the support of her friends in her Interweave MBS/Self-Reliance group, Deborah has been able to double her income in just a few weeks. Her family now has sufficient to eat!

She was contacted and trained by fellow Congolese "Success Ambassadors" in the informal sector for practically no cost and is meeting with a group of fellow micro-business owners that are solving their own business, home and community challenges through their MBS/Self-reliance groups.

The three intersecting areas of Self-Reliance

MBS/Self-reliance groups "interweave" income generating activities with home and community action. It provides a structure whereby people can help each other become more self-sufficient.

WHAT IS A "MASTERS OF BUSINESS IN THE STREET" MBS/SELF–RELIANCE GROUP?

Success in a micro-business is often interwoven with issues at home and in the community. If the family business is doing well but the father is an alcoholic and drinks the profits, success is elusive. If the micro-business is doing well and the family is working together but there is crime in the neighborhood and garbage in the streets, then self-sufficiency is difficult. People become more self-sufficient when they successfully interweave business, home and community efforts.

People earn a Masters of Business in the Street (MBS) Certificate when they join an MBS/Self-reliance group and complete all the course requirements. These groups usually consist of 5-15 people who have a desire to become self-sufficient. They earn the MBS by participating in 14 weekly classes led by a local Success Ambassador. Each week they learn a new business concept, set weekly commitments and report on how they implemented last week's goals in their businesses, homes and communities.

The classes are organized as a council in which the group members discuss real life case studies. They learn leadership skills as they discuss how to price, produce and promote their own products or services based on their local market. They address local challenges in the neighborhood and develop solutions. They support each other.

If after the 14-week class session they achieve all of the requirements and are approved by our international staff, they receive an MBS certificate from Interweave Solutions. The graduates then have the option to set a schedule to meet regularly to act as a mini chamber of commerce of the neighborhood to solve local business problems such as garbage in the street or delinquency. They hold each other accountable for

An MBS graduation at a school near Otavalo, Ecuador

ongoing commitments and can bring in guest speakers and resources from the community as needed.

Because business, home and community are so interwoven, plans are needed in all three areas to help a person become truly self-reliant. An MBS graduate develops and implements a business, home and community plan.

THE 6P'S OF BUSINESS

Unfortunately, jobs are hard to find in developing countries. There are few large corporations with formal jobs that provide regular wages and benefits. Nearly half the world, over three billion people, lives on less than $2.50 a day.

For many people, developing their own form of income is the only answer. However, they don't see themselves as small business owners. They are just trying to survive.

I don't have my own business. I just sell tortillas.

I need a job. At the moment, I just paint and fix people's houses to survive.

I don't keep records. I just sell bananas.

A church leader in Zimbabwe revealed that 95 percent of his local congregation was without formal work. "They live on what they can sell in the street, get from the church, or receive by begging. I must have people knocking on my door seeking assistance every two to three hours every day."

If there is no way to develop a small source of income, the people must rely on government, churches, and other non-governmental organizations (NGOs) for survival. Resorting to begging and sometimes stealing can be forms of income that some may use if they don't have a valid or dependable income. If a family member is successful in a business, often many other extended family members expect him or her to support them as well.

A family must have a source of income in order to be self-reliant and escape poverty. For many the answer is self-employment.

Some of Interweave's initial business training occurred in Uganda. We had been asked to meet with a neighborhood group in the outskirts of Kampala, close to the banks of Lake Victoria. Our task was to teach people small-business techniques.

I had reviewed my notes from my business training and recalled the curriculum I used in the Organizational Behavior classes I taught at the University of Nebraska in Kearney. My colleague reviewed his material from his MBA work at Brigham Young University. We had organized several PowerPoint slides that could be used as visual aids.

Our cultural ignorance could not have been more dramatic. We found ourselves in a thatched-roof structure that had bamboo sides and open-air windows. No electricity. The chickens that belonged to the owner providing the space had to be removed from the tables, and the wooden benches were crammed into every conceivable corner available.

The scent of the pigs, and their occasional squeals, came from the back, where they awaited slaughter less than ten yards away.

Then the people came. Dressed for a major event, the ladies were wearing beautiful homemade gowns that were obviously used only on special occasions. The men were scrubbed clean, and all were hungry for any information they could get from the educated trainers from the United States.

Many could not read. Others had only the basics of English, and it was a struggle to understand anything we said, let alone the S.W.O.T. analysis or strategic-planning material we had prepared. We were ready to present a first-world business program in a classroom lecture format to a developing country audience that could barely speak English and had no electricity. It was obvious that we were not going to reach our group, and we didn't.

We decided we had to rethink and rewrite how we teach business and self-reliance in developing nations. How could we simplify the complicated material taught in the universities and MBA programs around the world?

We started with the 6P's.

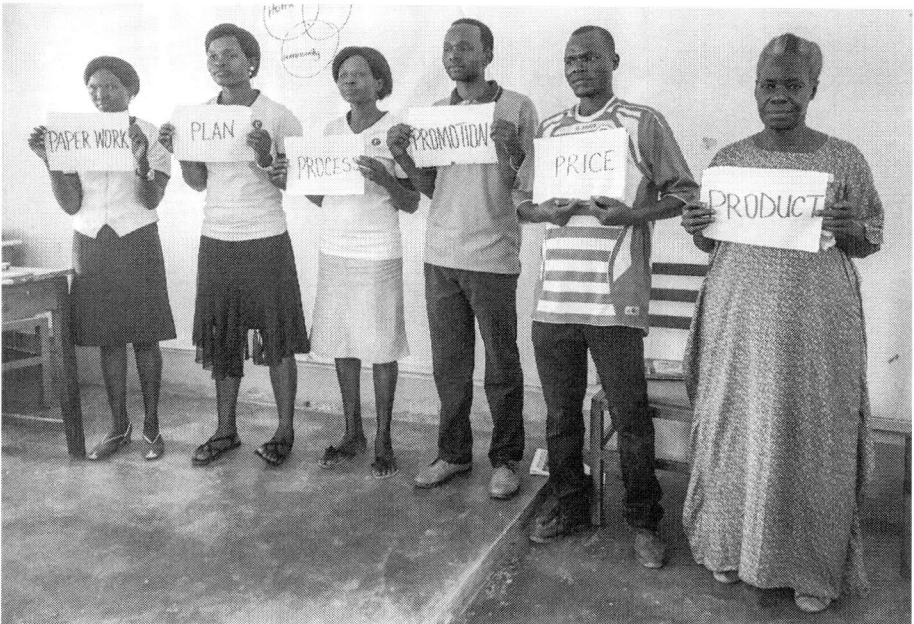

Learning the 6P's in Uganda

We divided all of the essential principles of small business into six areas of focus that we call **The 6P's of Business**.

- **Plan**
- **Product**
- **Process**
- **Price**
- **Promotion**
- **Paperwork**

Underneath each of these P's we have chosen five or six simple principles to guide the new entrepreneur.

The 6P's curriculum is a powerful tool to teach small-business principles. It does not depend on technology, and lay trainers can teach it. The 6P's training allows MBS/Self-reliance groups to develop their income by providing field-tested business principles in an easy-to-understand format. Step one in developing self-sufficiency is helping families secure an income by starting or improving their own micro-businesses, especially in areas where there are very few formal jobs.

Thousands of people worldwide have now implemented the 6P's of Business in their micro-businesses.

> *"I am keeping records for the first time."*

> *"I have a promotion plan and it's working!"*

> *"I am finally growing my business instead of just surviving!"*

The 6P's have helped people all over the world simplify the complex world of business and implement simple yet valuable business principles.

A study we did in Uganda reported a 64% increase in income by those who participated in Interweave's MBS program.

QUALITY OF LIFE AT HOME

The second circle to obtain self-sufficiency is to improve the quality of life in the home.

I was a little intimidated as I came to a straw home in central Mexico looking for Miguel Hernandez *(name changed)*. I had heard that he had been a very successful businessman in his day. He had organized the local indigenous population in that small mountain town in Mexico. He had a large family that had been a major influence in that poor village.

The house compound consisted of three straw rooms, covered with thatched roofs from the local banana plants. Cooking was done on a fire located in the open, in the center of the three straw structures. His wife, Maria, hovered over the fire making tortillas, placing them on the pan heated by the open fire made from the firewood that she had gathered that day.

She was shy and withdrawn. I asked her if Miguel was home, and with a fearful glance she mumbled, "I hope not."

It was Sunday morning and Saturday night had been rough for everyone. Miguel had been drinking again and apparently had been violent on his return home. Maria was dutifully fixing breakfast for the remaining children at home, but as I looked more closely, I saw that she had bruises and other signs of abuse.

"We are all afraid of him," she whispered. "We can do nothing without fear of his retaliation and anger. If you do find him, he will be at a bar or at another woman's house."

Miguel had been a successful businessman. That had all been lost, and now his family lived in fear and poverty, and he was a broken man.

GIVING CAN HURT

If one gets an income and wastes it on alcohol, does not educate his or her children, or abuses the family, then, ultimately, the family will be in poverty and be dependent on the mercy of others.

Poverty reduction and self-reliance come when the person and the family are setting and accomplishing personal and family goals.

CREATING BALANCE IN OUR LIVES

- What do you see in this picture?

- Why is the boy frustrated?

- Would you be frustrated in a similar situation?

- Have you ever been in a similar situation?

- Can you share that with the group?

Just like the boy with the square wheel, we can also become frustrated if our lives are not well rounded.

The questions you see above are an introduction to the MBS program, encouraging members of the groups to discuss their own personal quality of life. It is fascinating to listen as people talk of their struggles with family relationships, not being able to read, or their battles with alcohol. Some talk of losing weight or exercising regularly. The participants identify eight areas of life in which a person can consider improvement and then they rate themselves in each area.

Making a Quality-of-Life Wheel

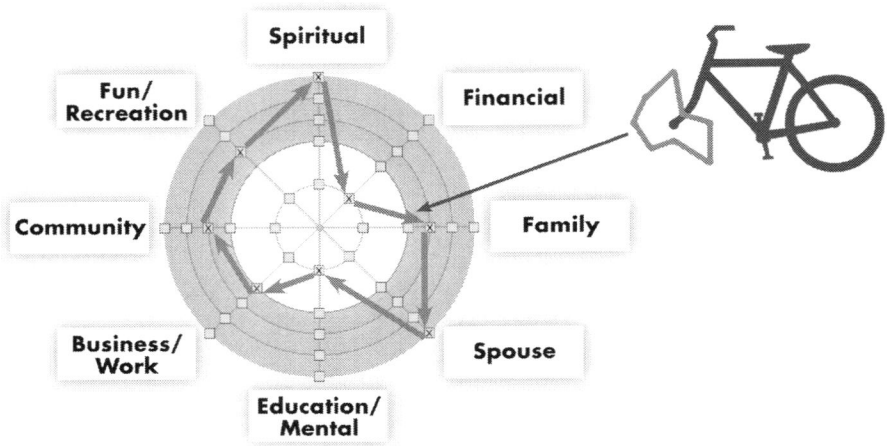

Quality-of-Life Wheel | *Is your life in balance?*

A rating close to the center of the circle means there is room for improvement. Marking the box on the outer edge of the circle suggests they are doing better in that area.

We then ask them to connect the dots. The connected dots will usually create a lop-sided circle, as shown in this example. The deformed circle represents the imbalance that the person may have in his or her life. We compare the deformed circle to the boy with the square-wheeled tricycle and invite members to set short-term and long-term goals on how to improve the balance in their lives.

Rodrigo was a member of a self-reliance group in Quito, Ecuador. He had started different businesses several times in his life. As he was making his Quality of Life plan he listed health as one of the areas of his life that he wanted to improve. He had a problem with alcohol and he realized that it didn't matter how well he could do business if he wasted all of his money and time drinking. He and his wife were separated and he knew that alcohol had destroyed his marriage. He decided to get help that week so he could stop drinking for good.

Each week he set another short-term goal to help him con-quer the drinking habit. He would not go to the bar with his friends this week, or would attend church that Sunday. He had a group to support him and ask him how he was doing each week. Working with the group on his personal goals, Rodrigo was able to take on the real cause of his poverty and save his marriage in the process.

Some members of the groups choose to improve their reading; others work on physical areas of their lives. Many set goals to have better communication in the home and to improve their education.

As people set personal goals, they begin to focus on a bal-anced life and not just how to make more money in a busi-ness. Self-reliance comes when the group members help each other in all three areas of business, home, and community. Home and life plans are an important part of that process.

HUNDREDS OF COMMUNITY SERVICE PROJECTS

In the mountains of Ecuador surrounding the beautiful capital of Quito, there is a garden. This garden used to be an empty field growing weeds and collecting wind-tossed garbage from the nearby community. Its owner, Gabriella, was an overwhelmed woman who didn't have the time, knowledge, or ability to clear and plant the space.

She joined an MBS/Self-Reliance Group. After a few meetings, members discussed the need for community service. They realized that self-reliance would occur only if they, as a community, began to resolve their own problems. During the group meeting, they listed some of the issues that were challenging the community. They discussed garbage in the streets, hungry children begging at the nearby plaza, reading problems, and poverty.

Suddenly, Gabriella spoke up. She owned land. If the self-reliance group wanted to use it, they could grow some food and share it with the local orphanage. The idea began to take shape, and before the night was over, the members had decided on a community service plan with specific dates and times to gather, plant and care for the garden.

They were successful, and six months later they had a productive harvest that they shared with those who participated in the work, in addition to a significant portion of the food going to the local orphanage.

Many social ills need to be resolved locally. International NGOs can plan from a distance to ship in food, build schools, or solve malaria, but real success comes when the local people decide what is a challenge to them and work together to overcome that challenge.

I have seen many water pumps in Africa that are broken and deserted, with people walking past them to the stream miles away. When I ask why they don't use the well, they simply explain that it doesn't work. Foreigners came, dug and built a well, and left. It worked for a while, and then it broke.

"We don't know how to fix it," they say. "We didn't build it," they reason, and "We don't know who is responsible for it."

The attitude of some people in certain communities is to appear to foreigners as poor and as helpless as possible, so that the international NGOs will see that they need the well (school, bridge, dental help) more than the other communities.

Luck and hope for an international intervention is not the way to create self-reliance. Ideas and plans must come from the community members. When they form groups to discuss local problems, the need for a school or a well, then they can work to achieve it.

When together they dig their own well or build their own school there is a sense of self-reliance. If they don't have the initial money or knowledge they need to accomplish their goal, they learn where to find it. They ask questions, they save money, they offer their labor, and they contact resources. They do all they can to help themselves and to resolve their own problems.

If they have the opportunity to partner with an international NGO, then they will already have the organization and plan to maintain the well or school when it is built.

Community-based service projects generated by the local neighborhood are powerful ways to increase self-reliance and reduce poverty.

Community problems can often get in the way of successful micro-businesses or quality-of-life goals. In Marimba Park, a humble area outside Harare in Zimbabwe, there is a local elementary school that serves the community. There is a lot of land surrounding the school building, making a great place for the kids to play. However, the land is covered with tall grass and therein lies the problem.

The school doesn't have lawn mowers or grass cutters to clear out the grass, so it just grows. The tall grass makes a fun place for kids to play, but also a great place for snakes to thrive.

Service Project in Zimbabwe | *Clearing overgrown grass around the school*

The parents, worried about the snakes and the danger to the kids, were hesitant to send their children to school. This affected their ability to run their small businesses and to achieve the goal of educating their children.

In an MBS/Self-reliance meeting, members identified the problem and arranged a solution. One Saturday morning, prior to their local group training on the 6P's of Business, they donned matching T-shirts, walked the mile from where they were meeting to the elementary school, and attacked the tall grass.

Each parent had a slasher, a small golf club-like tool with a sickle attached to the end instead of a nine iron. They cut and slashed for an hour until the tall grass was down and then returned to their meeting place and began to train each other on small-business techniques.

Many times, people in developing countries can't depend on local community services. Garbage, lack of streetlights, and insufficient police protection are just some of the many problems that can affect the quality of life and the success of the local businesses. When a community is taught to be self-reliant and is given the structure and support to make it happen, the citizens can solve many of their local problems.

For example, Marie attended a self-reliance group in Kinshasa, Congo. She hoped to grow and improve her grain selling business. Marie became quite successful applying the 6P's of business. She even added catering to her efforts. Her income increased substantially. She soon found that just increasing her business profits wasn't enough. She worried about the orphans living on the streets in her community. Taking the meager profits she earned from her business and involving people in her community, she created an orphanage and a school for the children she saw living in the streets. Marie now lives in that sweet spot of self-reliance where her businesses flourish, her personal life is happy and orphans in her community enjoy a place to sleep, eat and receive an education.

Self-reliance occurs when good people (rich or poor) are doing all they can to solve their own problems. In order to do that, the community must meet and discuss the local issues. MBS/ Self-reliance groups facilitate this cooperation by encouraging and teaching people to create and implement plans in their own business, home and community.

Self-reliance is attainable when individuals and their communities unite to teach each other business techniques, help each other set personal short and long-term goals, and work together to solve local community problems.

SUCCESS AMBASSADORS

We move people from poverty to prosperity through neighborhood MBS/Self-reliance groups.

—Interweave Solutions Mission Statement

MBS/Self-reliance groups transform the way the world fights poverty. Through these groups, millions of people will have higher income, better homes and improved communities.

—Interweave Solutions Vision Statement

Our vision is to have millions of people earn an MBS certificate and be part of an MBS/self-reliance group. That is only possible if thousands of people are trained on how to offer and facilitate MBS/self-reliance groups. We do that through Success Ambassadors.

Success Ambassadors are motivated people that want to start their own small training business in their local area. They become a Success Ambassador by taking two courses: the full MBS course, and the Success Ambassador course. Through this process they learn how to create MBS/self-reliance groups.

The curriculum was originally written and designed for street-smart but formally uneducated micro-business owners. However, we have found that entrepreneurs and students of all ages can benefit from earning an MBS certificate and being part of an MBS/Self-reliance group.

Wayne Barrow is a Success Ambassador in Guyana. Interweave contracted with him while implementing a consulting contract to set up self-reliance groups for a church in Guyana. When the six-month contract ended with Interweave, he was about to become unemployed again. We asked him if he would like to contact other churches, government agencies and NGOs to see if they would be interested in offering MBS/Self-reliance groups to the people in their organizations.

Wayne contacted several people and finally was able to connect with the First Lady of Guyana who wanted to provide a service to their country. She contracted with Wayne to offer the Interweave model to people throughout Guyana. He is now paid to implement Inteweave MBS/Self-reliance groups. The Guyana Small Business Administration saw his work and they also made a contract with him. He is not an employee of Interweave. He runs his own business training people how to start and grow their businesses and become more self-reliant.

Chio, a Success Ambassador in Quito, Ecuador, has trained Micro-Finance Institutions, Government Agencies and local churches how to create MBS/Self-reliance groups and receive MBS certificates. She has her own business and offers the MBS certificate as one of her products. As a certified Success Ambassador, she has authorization to print and offer the MBS program. She becomes more self-reliant as she helps others.

Yasmina from Cartagena, Colombia, is a teacher at a local school in a poor neighborhood. Her husband left her and she needed extra income to support her children. As a Success Ambassador, she offers the MBS program to the parents of her students and is paid by a foundation that is committed to improve the education of people in that area. Not only does Yasmina earn extra income, but the parents start and grow their businesses, which makes it easier to pay the educational expenses of their children. In addition, the foundation is meeting its mission to improve the education of parents and children!

Success Ambassadors are people who want to help their community, and at the same time earn some money themselves by offering MBS/Self-reliance groups to individuals or organizations who want to start or have their participants start and grow their own micro-businesses.

A Success Ambassador conference in South America

SUCCESS AMBASSADORS AS A BUSINESS MODEL

When local motivated people become Success Ambassadors they can charge others for the MBS certificate and offer it to churches, governments, NGOs, Finance Institutions or neighbors. Some facilitate MBS/Self-reliance groups part-time to supplement their income and others have turned it into a success full-time business for themselves and others.

The Success Ambassadors offer the MBS to their community and charge a competitive price depending what the market will pay. The price differs from one area to another.

Yasmin from Soacha, Colombia, a poorer community near Bogota, charged $15 for a local group she organized with her neighbors. Alex, a Success Ambassador in Quito, Ecuador charged group members $40 for an MBS course. Price depends on the local market and that varies worldwide.

The Success Ambassadors are equipped with training, a curriculum and the certification of Interweave Solutions, an International NGO. No office is needed because the Ambassador will go to the people or organization instead of the people coming to a central office. Success Ambassadors give of their time and really have an impact by organizing their own businesses and helping others do the same.

Sometimes Success Ambassadors can receive grants from Interweave's generous donors, to help them print materials, legalize their business or help with transportation. Our end goal is that Success Ambassadors become self-sufficient by creating a business or organization that assists others in becoming self-sufficient as well.

Success Ambassadors can also be employees of a church, school, government agency or NGO. The organization makes a contract with an Interweave Success Ambassador to train their staff. Their staff then earns their MBS and some of their staff members can become Success Ambassadors. The agency can then offer the MBS program in their local area.

To start an MBS group, the Success Ambassador either works with a partner organization who announces the new program to its members, or they find their own clients through family, friends or online or community marketing. The Success Ambassador recruits clients by explaining that a group is being formed to help anyone who is interested start or improve their micro-business and be more successful in life.

All the interested members in that organization or neighborhood meet for an orientation where the Interweave MBS/Self-reliance model is explained. They are invited to the group meetings to be held once or twice a week to earn their Masters of Business in the Street (MBS) certificate. The Success Ambassador sets up different days and times for each of the organizations or groups that they will facilitate.

It is more than just a class. It is a commitment to improve a person's business, home, and community. The objective is to support and encourage people as they make important life changes.

After three to five meetings, the group will know which members are attending regularly and showing leadership potential. In one of the meetings, members have an election of group leaders who will help plan, organize and eventually teach the material and keep the group itself meeting.

The Ambassador begins to mentor the leadership of the group. The groups decide topics to discuss and organize the community service projects. The Ambassador and the group leaders begin to identify people who can provide insight and training within the group. The curriculum materials are shared with the group, and the members of the group begin to teach the lessons, lead the discussions, and decide the future efforts of the group all while earning the MBS certificate.

Upon graduation with the MBS certificate, the groups are often functioning on their own. The organization or neighborhood has its own self-reliance group with MBS graduates. The Success Ambassador's role is now to encourage group members to continue meeting regularly to hold each other accountable and continue progressing.

Now the organization is self-reliant in helping its members. It is not waiting for an outside agency or government to solve its problems. The congregation or organization has the structure and capability to help itself.

Success Ambassadors have now established MBS/Self-Reliance groups with churches of many faiths, schools, micro-finance institutions, government agencies, drug rehabilitation centers and even businesses that want their employees to be entrepreneurs and sell their products. Self-Reliance groups work.

One study showed that after taking the MBS course:

- 76% of participants started keeping business records.
- 90% of participants improved their personal savings.
- 93% reported that their income had increased.
- 97% said they had a plan to improve their quality of life.

Success Ambassadors can use the MBS/Self Reliance program to provide a system so that people help themselves. With a tested curriculum and a group format in which people can counsel together to solve personal and local problems the Success Ambassador earns money while helping their country, one group of micro-business owners at a time.

An MBS Class in the street in Ecuador

KNOWLEDGE FIRST;
THEN MONEY

One of the questions we hear the most is, "Do you provide loans? I can't start my business if I don't have money."

Our experience over many years is that money does not come first. In order to succeed, the business knowledge comes first.

THE LANGUAGE OF BUSINESS

In 2010 I visited a group of people interested in starting a business in Zimbabwe. When they heard a North American was coming they must have assumed I was bringing money, because as soon as we started the meeting they presented me with their business plans.

There were about twenty different plans. They ranged from taxi businesses to restaurants, and travel agencies to fumigation services. They were asking for thousands of dollars to buy the taxis, equip the restaurants and provide all of the needed capital to start their plans.

They were excellent business plans. They were typed and had all of the correct jargon; market share, cash projections, strength, weakness, opportunities & theats analysis, etc. They must have had a class on business plans. Some were probably professionally written.

"Can you show me your business records, income statements and cash projections?" I asked them.

"Do you know how to improve your market share or work with employees?"

When I asked them if they had any experience running a business or if they had invested time or money in testing their ideas, they said no.

"We don't have any money. We can't start a business. Give us money and we will learn how to run a business."

I responded, "If you want to talk about money you need to know the language of money. Show me your income statements for the past six-months; show me your cash projections for the coming year. Show me your plans on systems improvement (process), pricing and promotion ideas and product innovations."

If they can show their paperwork for even a chewing gum business or a banana stand, it shows the investor that the potential business owner knows the concepts and is perhaps ready for a loan.

I visited a dry-cleaning business owner in the Congo who said he needed more money. When I entered the shop, it was dirty and the clothes to be cleaned were in a pile on the floor.

I asked him about his process for taking orders and keeping track of customer's clothes. He had none.

I asked to see his paperwork. He had none.

I asked about any promotion plans for rewarding loyal customers or getting new ones. He had none.

I asked how he arrived at his pricing plan and what the competition charged. He didn't know.

I asked him what he would spend more money on if he got the loan. He wasn't sure.

It was obvious to me that the last thing this business owner needed was more debt. Until he applied the 6P's (Plan, Product, Processes, Price, Promotion and Paperwork) into his existing business, more money would just mask the problems his business needed to solve. If he could improve the 6P's in his business he might not need to get a loan at all.

If a micro business owner can speak the language of money, has some experience and knows exactly what productive assets the borrowed money will buy, then, perhaps, they are ready for a loan. If not, they need MBS training first.

As a potential investor, I wouldn't risk my money on people with no knowledge of basic business principles. It is one thing to write a business plan. It is another to have business experience. They need both.

Business knowledge and experience comes before debt and loans, not the other way around.

Maria has been making children's underwear for fifteen years. She has two sewing machines in a room in the back of her family's humble home in Quito, Ecuador. For the last fifteen years Maria has struggled to have enough material to get ahead. With the little amount she makes, she buys small amounts of material, makes some clothes, sells them, and buys a little more material to repeat the process.

Maria also never kept books. If she sold an undergarment and had the money in her pocket, it was available money. If the children wanted school supplies or food was needed then the money would be used. She never was sure how much money she made and never seemed to get ahead.

Then Maria joined an MBS/Self-reliance group. For the first time in fifteen years, she began to record her business income and expenses. She separated her business and personal money, and she began to brand her products. Maria was no longer selling underwear; she was selling "Daisy" undergarments for women and "Tom Steel" briefs for men. Demand began to increase.

Maria was in a position to expand the business and really make it grow, but she needed capital. With a business loan, she could buy more material at a cheaper price, buy labels for her garments, and put them in designed boxes instead of cheap plastic bags. She needed money, and she was prepared to invest it. She obtained a loan from a local micro finance institution.

When loans and financing make sense, they come after the MBS 6P's training. One of the units of the MBS course is to know the four guidelines in getting a loan: the **terms** of the loan, the correct **amount** needed to implement a specific plan, the **motive** for the loan and the **timing** of the loan. Many people who start the MBS saying they needed money, end the course deciding that they can grow the business in a better way than going into more debt.

OBTAINING CREDIT

One of the biggest challenges that come with micro-business development is how to obtain the money to start or grow the small business when they are ready for a loan.

Banks, especially in developing countries, generally do not make micro-business loans. They require a business to be already established, with profit and loss statements, collateral, and years of profitability. People with no formal business records, training, or assets are not a sensible business risk for a formal bank.

In the past thirty years, another financial institution has emerged called a micro-finance institution or MFI. Recognizing the need for smaller loans to new individuals, MFIs are organized to give micro-loans.

There are thousands of MFIs in the world. Almost every area of the world has access to at least one. In most areas of the world, there is competition for the best loans available. Each MFI has its own interest rate, fees, and payback plans. Each one has its own system of how it uses groups or how it uses collateral and credit scores. Understanding the structure of the local available MFIs is an important part of helping people become self-reliant.

Once a person has an MBS certificate, their first step to obtaining business capital is to know the MFIs in the local area and to evaluate each one. The Interweave Success Ambassadors train the group to study each MFI and try to make a relationship with one or two that can be beneficial to the individuals in the group. Of course, the group members should have a 6P's business plan and have analyzed the four guidelines for business debt.

The MFI can come to the group or vice versa, but when the MBS graduates talk to the finance institution, they know the language of money and are aware of the terms, amount, motive and timing for the loan.

Remember, training comes first and then the money, not the other way around.

People with an MBS certificate are in a much better position to get a loan, if they really need it.

WHAT IF THEY CAN'T READ OR SPEAK THE LANGUAGE?

Anita is a talented seamstress and mother of five children. She and her husband make their living farming and sewing in the mountains of Chiapas, Mexico. Her native language is Tzotzil and she struggles to speak Mexico's dominant language, Spanish. They are part of the 14 million indigenes in Mexico that struggle to read, speak and write in Spanish.

In the United States over 60 million people, 20% of US households, do not speak English as the prominent language in their home. Worldwide hundreds of millions of capable people try to earn a living unable to read or speak in the country's dominant language.

How do you offer the MBS to them?

It is harder to start a business when a person can't read or speak the nation's dominant language. However, it may be impossible for that person to find formal employment and buying and selling may be the only option. That is one of the reasons we see people selling candy bars on the buses and trains, juggling at the stop signs and selling gum on the corner in many countries. They are in the informal economy trying to survive.

A self-reliance group and MBS certificate would give them the ability to improve their street business, have a support group, learn how to make their business legal and improve their own homes and communities.

In order to reach people that don't read or speak the country's dominant language Interweave has developed materials in simple English and Spanish, (with more languages planned),

63

to help them learn those languages. At the same time they can start or improve a simple business so that they eventually can earn an MBS certificate and become self-sufficient.

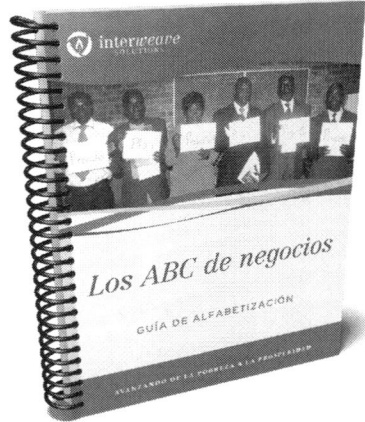

ABC's of Business in English and Spanish

The ABCs of Business teaches reading and speaking in English or Spanish at a beginning level. It is for refugees or English or Spanish second language learners that must eventually read the dominant language in order to start a simple business.

Instead of *A is for Apples and B is for Bananas* it gets right to business. A is for Assets and B is for Budgets. They discuss simple reading concepts in a business context.

These tools were written to help those who need to emphasize speaking English or Spanish as their business language. It discusses the 6P's of Business in a simple way so that they can learn how to speak the language while practicing business principles.

We used this manual with a group of non-English native speakers from Arabic speaking countries in Salt Lake City. They practiced their English while working on their own

English for Business Success! and Spanish for Business Success!

businesses. Several started new businesses and several more obtained the confidence in English to seek work. They set goals and began to learn the basics of the 6P's of Business.

Once they have used the reading and speaking tools mentioned, they are then ready to earn their MBS certificate. They have a vocabulary to discuss business concepts. They are ready to learn how to start and grow their own business.

These tools continue to be met with great success in Uganda and are currently being tested in Chiapas, Mexico and in refugee groups in Salt Lake City.

WHAT NEXT?

We encourage you to give. Be generous. But for at least part of your giving and/or part of your volunteer time, give to self-sufficiency.

Interweave Solutions is dedicated to helping people become self-reliant by recruiting, training and supporting Success Ambassadors. There are Success Ambassadors around the world facilitating MBS/self-reliance groups. In these groups hundreds of people are developing their businesses, homes and communities. We want it to be a million people in the next seven years.

Hairdressers, artisans, gardeners, shopkeepers, clothes makers and more have all improved their sources of income by learning and teaching the 6P's of Business. Record keeping, promotion plans, branding ideas, and pricing plans have all been implemented. Many have taught each other. Their classes are now ongoing in the community.

Personal goals are being set. People are becoming sober, attending church, and making peace with their spouses. People are saving money for the first time and are keeping personal budgets. The groups are helping individuals improve their own businesses, homes, and communities.

Service has included killing the snakes and cutting the grass in Zimbabwe to visiting old folk's homes in Ecuador. Orphanages are painted, streets are cleaned, and gardens grown and harvested, all in an effort to solve local problems without government or international involvement.

You can specifically help create self-reliance in four ways at Interweave Solutions.

An MBS group setting goals in Uganda

First, sponsor a Success Ambassador. Success Ambassadors often need money to get their MBS/Self-Reliance groups started, with needs such as transportation, printing, or making a legal business entity. With Interweave certification and the help of your grant, hundreds of people can be enabled to reach self-reliance by becoming Success Ambassadors in a country of your choice.

Second, sponsor an organization. We often get requests from organizations that hear about us in developing countries. They want to start groups but can't afford the materials and training. You could provide the funds to train Success Ambassadors in that organization.

We were once contacted by an NGO in Africa that needed help with self-reliance. Hundreds of girls had been kidnapped by rebel armies in Uganda. Used as sex slaves, these girls spent the next six years in the rebel camps. The war is now over and these young women with their children are being dumped and deserted on the roads of Uganda. The NGO wanted to help with immediate demands but needed a long-term plan for income generation for these families. Simple small business techniques, group support and goal setting through self-reliance groups should be an important part of that long-term strategy. You could provide an NGO like this with the supplies necessary to start those groups.

Third, provide a self-reliance scholarship. For very little money, a young mother in Tampico, Mexico or Kinshasa, Congo could earn an MBS certificate. Through the Interweave scholarship program, they can apply for the training that is offered by a local Success Ambassador. They pay something, even a small amount, to buy their workbooks, and then we give a scholarship payment to their Success Ambassador for the course.

The Ambassador develops groups and earns some money, the participant buys their books and studies, and your donation helps someone to be more self-sufficient.

A school in Choluteca, Honduras once contacted our local Success Ambassador. They wanted to train their 51 high school seniors but they couldn't afford materials. Through a scholarship contribution, similar to what we are asking from you, we provided materials for them to establish their own MBS/self-reliance group. Don't worry. We encouraged them to provide service to their community in order to earn that scholarship!

Finally, become a Success Ambassador. You can earn the MBS certificate and become a Success Ambassador with online and mentor training very inexpensively. No matter what country you are in there are people who need to improve their business, home and community. You or someone you know can become an agent of change. Become a Success Ambassador.

If you become a Success Ambassador, you will change people's lives as you help MBS self-reliance group members develop and implement their own business, home and community action plans.

IT CAN BE DONE

When you give with self-sufficiency in mind you will give differently. You will ask self-sufficiency questions and you will encourage and create hope as you actively discuss how people can earn what they need. It is harder than simply giving but it is more rewarding.

> You can help someone conquer their own poverty.
> Donate for self-sufficiency at
> **interweavesolutions.org/donate**
> and make a real difference.

Giving can hurt; but, when we give with self-sufficiency in mind, we can change lives. Let's work together, giving for impact, to help people lift themselves out of poverty.

ABOUT THE AUTHOR

Dean H. Curtis is the chairman and co-founder of Interweave Solutions, a non-profit organization that has created hundreds of MBS/Self-reliance groups worldwide.

Prior to creating Interweave Solutions, Dean was a successful entrepreneur who established and sold a business with over 500 employees, was a former Assistant Professor of Communication and Business at the University of Nebraska in Kearney, and taught high school in Spanish Fork, Utah.

Dean completed his Ph.D. coursework at the University of Nebraska, Lincoln (starting a business instead of writing a dissertation) and has a masters and bachelor's degree from Brigham Young University.

Dean and his wife have served their church with their family on a three-year mission to Tampico, Mexico and as a young man, Dean served a two-year mission in Argentina. They are the parents of nine children.

Dean has traveled worldwide, teaching principles of self-reliance.

Visit *interweavesolutions.org* to learn more.

53884742R00043

Made in the USA
Columbia, SC
22 March 2019